12606

EASY-READ FACT BOOKS

Dinosaurs

Andrew Langley

Franklin Watts

London · New York · Sydney · Toronto

© 1987 Franklin Watts

Franklin Watts
12a Golden Square
London W1

First published in the USA by
Franklin Watts Inc.
387 Park Avenue South
New York, N.Y. 10016

Franklin Watts Australia
14 Mars Road
Lane Cove
NSW 2066

Phototypeset by Keyspools
Limited
Printed in Hong Kong

UK ISBN: 0 86313 574 9

US ISBN 0–531–10449–4
Library of Congress Catalog
Card No: 87–61347

Photographs:
Imitor

Illustrations:
Christopher Forsey
Hayward Art Group
Michael Roffe

Design:
Janet King
David Jefferis

Technical consultant:
Beverley Halstead Ph D, DSc
Printed in Hong Kong

Note: The majority of illustrations
in this book originally appeared in
"Dinosaurs": An Easy Read Fact
Book.

Contents

Dinosaurs large and small

Dinosaurs were land animals that lived many millions of years ago. Their name means *terrible lizards.* The largest dinosaur would have weighed more than 1,500 people. The smallest was not much bigger than a blackbird.

Triceratops

Supersaurus

Diplodocus

Mussaurus

Tyrannosaurus　　**Compsognathus**　　5

Baby dinosaurs

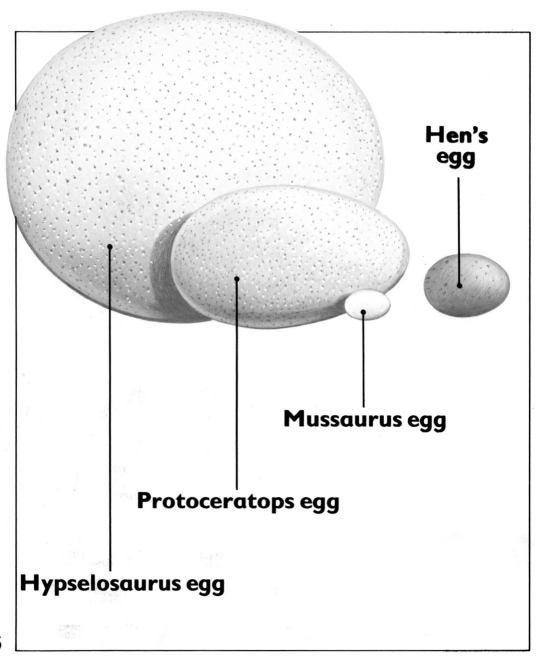

Hen's egg

Mussaurus egg

Protoceratops egg

Hypselosaurus egg

Baby dinosaurs hatched from eggs.
Some mothers laid their eggs in
hollows dug in the ground. Perhaps
the Sun's heat hatched them or
maybe the mothers warmed them.
Some babies stayed in the nest
while their mothers brought food.

Plant-eaters

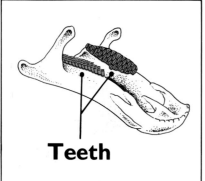

Teeth

The jaw of a duck-billed dinosaur. One dinosaur had 2,000 teeth.

Many dinosaurs ate only plants. The long, low ones fed on the shorter bushes. Horned dinosaurs chewed up tough leaves from palm trees. Some *sauropods* could reach the top leaves of tall trees.

The neck of the
Mamenchisaurus
was 33 ft (10 m)
long.

The teeth of the
Stytacosaurus
cut like scissors.

Flesh-eaters

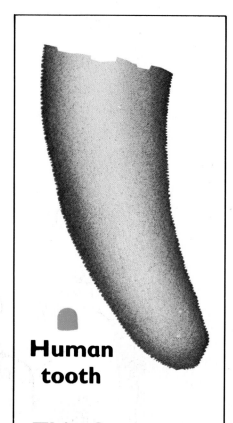

Human tooth

This *Carnosaur* tooth is only half its real size. It could cut flesh like a steak knife.

Killer or flesh-eating dinosaurs fed on the plant-eaters. They had sharp teeth and claws to help them slice through skin and flesh.

A *Deinonychus* attacks a plant-eating Iguanodon.

11

Defense and escape

Some plant-eaters were easily killed but many had ways to defend themselves. Dinosaurs like *Stegosaurus* grew bony plates or spines to protect themselves. Triceratops had three long horns to use as weapons. Small dinosaurs used their speed to escape from danger.

Ornithomimus could sprint faster than its enemies.

Scolosaurus could only move slowly, but had thick bony armour.

Triceratops had three long horns and a bony frill around the neck.

Masters of sea and sky

Reptiles also ruled the sea and air. Giant *plesiosaurs* swam with legs shaped like paddles. *Pterosaurs* flapped or glided overhead on wings of skin.

The mosasaur *Tylosaurus* was a giant water lizard that crunched up shell fish.

The pleisosaur *Hydrotherosaurus* lived in shallow seas and caught fish.

The pterosaur *Quetzalcoatlus* may have been the largest flying animal ever.

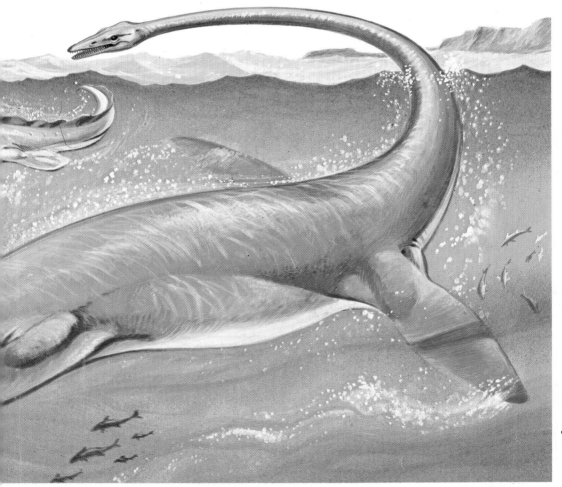

15

Keeping warm

Most dinosaurs needed to be warm before they could move around. They got their heat from the Sun. At night they grew cold again, just as snakes and lizards do today.

Spinosaurus had a skin sail which helped to cool it down.

Scientists now think that some dinosaurs may have been warm-blooded like mammals today. They could make their own heat.

Small dinosaurs like these *Compsognathus* may have grown feathers to keep warm. The huge *Apatosaurus* lost heat very slowly.

Dinosaurs on the move

Dinosaurs with armor and horns always walked on all fours. The flesh-eaters walked and ran on their long hind legs. Some dinosaurs had webbed toes and could also swim.

Megalosaurus

Apatasaurus

Megalosaurus was a big flesh eating dinosaur. *Hypsilophodon* was small and agile. *Apatosaurus* could swim as well as walk on land.

Hypsilophodon

19

Where and when they lived

Ankylosaurus
lived about 100
million years
ago.

**Evidence of
dinosaurs has been
found in most
parts of the world.
Some lived on hills
and some on low
plains. Most
preferred the warm
lush forests that
covered large areas
of the Earth.**

Keutrosaurus
lived over 150
million years
ago.

The Age of Dinosaurs lasted for 140 million years, but the different types of dinosaur lived for only a few million years. Some types died out and new ones appeared.

Stegosaurus lived over 150 million years ago.

Death of the dinosaurs

About sixty-five million years ago all the dinosaurs died out. Nobody is quite sure why. Perhaps they ran out of food. The climate may have become too hot for them. Scientists are still trying to find out the true reasons for the disappearance of the dinosaurs.

After the dinosaurs

The relatives of the dinosaurs can still be found today. Crocodiles and alligators come from the same group of reptiles as dinosaurs. Even birds may be related to them. The *Archaeopteryx* may have been the first bird. It had feathers and could probably fly. It is very like the small *Compsognathus*.

Compsognathus

24

Archaeopteryx

Crocodiles behave very much like their prehistoric cousins. They are low on the ground and can run fast for short distances.

The **9,000** kinds of birds alive today could be descendants of dinosaurs who died out 65 million years ago.

Fossil dinosaurs

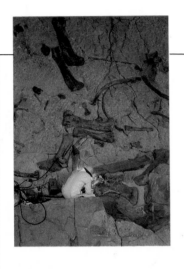

Fossil bones at the Dinosaur National Monument in Utah USA.

Most dead dinosaurs just rotted away and left no remains. Some sank in water. Their bones were covered in mud and became fossils. Fossil hunters collect such bones and take them to museums. Experts can fit bones together and rebuild a dinosaur skeleton.

The dinosaur family tree

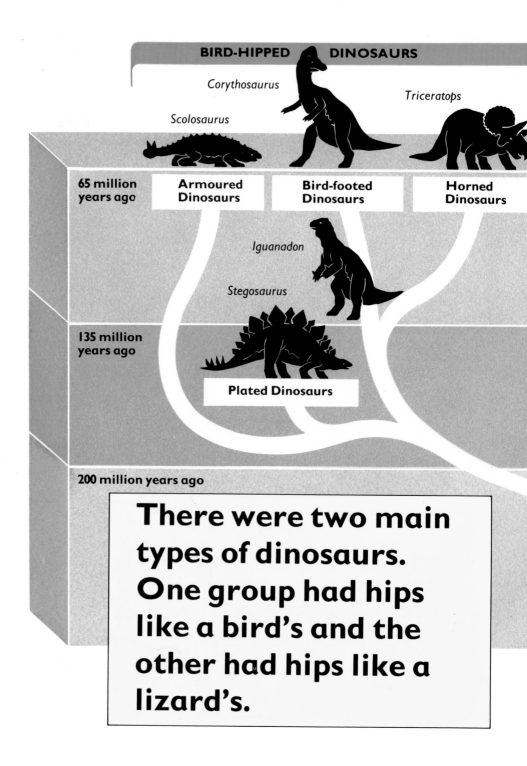

BIRD-HIPPED DINOSAURS

Corythosaurus

Triceratops

Scolosaurus

| 65 million years ago | Armoured Dinosaurs | Bird-footed Dinosaurs | Horned Dinosaurs |

Iguanadon

Stegosaurus

| 135 million years ago | | | |

Plated Dinosaurs

200 million years ago

There were two main types of dinosaurs. One group had hips like a bird's and the other had hips like a lizard's.

LIZARD-HIPPED DINOSAURS

Dromaeosaurus

Tyrannosaurus

Ornithomimus

Alamosaurus

Deinonychids **Coeluvosaurs** **Carnosaurs** **Sauropods**

Deinonychus

Megalosaurus

Compsognathus

Ceolophysis

Brachiosaurus

Plateosaurus

Prosauropods

All dinosaurs may have had the same reptile ancestors.

29

How to say the names

Alamosaurus
(a-LAM-oe-sawr-us)
Ankylosaur
(an-KIL-oe-sawr)
Apatosaurus
(a-PA-toe-saw-rus)
Archaeopteryx
(are-kay-OP-terix)
Brachiosaurus
(brak-ee-oe-SAW-rus)
Coelophysis
(seal-o-FI-sis)
Coelurosaur
(SEAL-ur-o-sawr)
Compsognathus
(comp-sog-NATH-us)
Corythosaurus
(cor-ITH-o-sawr-us)
Deinonychus
(dine-o-NIKE-us)
Diplodocus
(dip-LOD-o-kus)
Hydrotherosaurus
(hide-ro-ther-o-SAW-rus)
Hypselosaurus
(hip-sel-o-SAW-rus)
Hypsilophodon
(hip-si-LOF-o-don)
Kentrosaurus
(KEN-tro-saw-rus)
Maiasaura
(my-a-SAWR-a)

Mamenchisaurus
(ma-men-ki-SAW-rus)
Megalosaurus
(megal-o-SAWR-us)
Mussaurus
(mus-SAW-rus)
Ornithomimus
(orn-ee-thoe-MIME-us)
Plateosaurus
(plat-ee-o-SAW-rus)
Plesiosaur
(PLEE-see-o-sawr)
Protoceratops
(proe-toe-SERA-tops)
Pterosaur
(TER-o-sawr)
Quetzalcoatlus
(kwet-zal-koe-AT-lus)
Sauropod
(SAWR-o-pod)
Scolosaurus
(skol-o-SAWR-us)
Spinosaurus
(spine-oe-SAW-rus)
Stegosaurus
(STEG-o-sawr-us)
Triceratops
(try-SER-a-tops)
Tylosaurus
(TY-lo-sawr-us)
Tyrannosaurus
(tie-ran-oe-SAW-rus)

Glossary

Here is the meaning of some of the words used in this book:

Ankylosaur

"Stiff lizard" – dinosaur with short legs and bony covering.

Apatosaur

A huge plant-eating dinosaur also known as Brontosaurus.

Archaeopteryx

A feathered dinosaur which is thought to be the first bird-like animal.

Composognathus

'With a slender jaw' – a reptile which looked very like a bird.

Deinonychids

"Terrible claws" – fierce flesh-eating dinosaurs.

Fossil

The remains of an animal or plant which is preserved in rock.

Ornithomimus

"Like a bird" – a small dinosaur with long legs and neck.

Plesiosaur

A reptile which lived in the sea.

Pterosaur

A reptile which glided or flew.

Sauropod

"Lizard-footed" – the largest dinosaur of all.

Stegosaur

"Plated monster" – a dinosaur with armored plates or spines on its back.

Triceratops

A dinosaur with three horns.

Tyrannosaur

A huge flesh-eating dinosaur which stood on its hind legs.

31

Index